Famous Places of the World

Africa

Helen Bateman and Jayne Denshire

Smart Apple Media

This edition first published in 2006 in the United States of America by Smart Apple Media.

Smart Apple Media
2140 Howard Drive West
North Mankato
Minnesota 56003

First published in 2006 by
MACMILLAN EDUCATION AUSTRALIA PTY LTD
627 Chapel Street, South Yarra, Australia 3141

Visit our Web site at www.macmillan.com.au

Associated companies and representatives throughout the world.

Copyright © Helen Bateman and Jayne Denshire 2006

Library of Congress Cataloging-in-Publication Data

Bateman, Helen.
    Africa / by Helen Bateman and Jayne Denshire.
    p. cm. — (Famous places of the world)
    Includes index.
    ISBN-13: 978-1-58340-799-8 (alk. paper)
    1. Africa—Juvenile literature. 2. Africa—Geography—Juvenile literature.
    I. Denshire, Jayne. II. Title.

    DT3B38 2006
    960—dc22   2006002519

Project management by Limelight Press Pty Ltd
Design by Stan Lamond, Lamond Art & Design
Illustrations by Marjorie Crosby-Fairall
Maps by Lamond Art & Design and Andrew Davies
Map icons by Andrew Davies
Research by Kathy Gerrard
Consultant: Colin Sale BA (Sydney) MSc (London)

Printed in USA

Acknowledgments
The authors and the publisher are grateful to the following for permission to reproduce copyright material:

Cover photograph: Sphinx and Great Pyramid at Giza, courtesy of iStockphoto/John Snelgrove. GettyImages/Daryl Balfour p. 26; GettyImages/Bruno Morandi p. 25; iStockphoto/Georg v.Breitenbuch p. 4 (left); iStockphoto/Harry Boden pp. 4 (center right), 15; iStockphoto/Klaas Lingbeek-van Kranen p. 29; iStockphoto/Ogen Perry p. 4 (right); iStockphoto p. 11 (bottom right); iStockphoto/Steven Tilston p. 11 (top); Lonely Planet/Juliet Coombe p. 7; Lonely Planet/Grant Dixon p. 27; Lonely Planet/Donald C. & Priscilla Alexander Eastman p. 9; Lonely Planet/Lee Foster p. 20; Lonely Planet/Dennis Johnson p. 18; Lonely Planet/Chris Mellor p. 16; Lonely Planet/ Ariadne Van Zandbergen pp. 19 (top left), 28; Lonely Planet/Wayne Walton p. 12; PhotoDisc p. 10; Photolibrary.com/INC SUPERSTOCK p. 13; Photolibrary.com/Stan Osolinski p. 14; Photolibrary. com/Doug Scott p. 23 (bottom left); Photolibrary.com/Rick Strange p. 19 (bottom right); Photolibrary. com/The Travel Library p. 17 (top right); Photolibrary.com/Ariadne Van Zandbergen p. 24; Colin Sale, Atlas Picture Library pp. 4 (center left), 6, 8, 17 (center left), 21, 22, 23 (center right).

Contents

When a word in the text is printed in **bold**. You can look up its meaning in the Glossary on page 31.

Wonders of Africa

Africa is the world's second largest **continent**. Much of its centre is covered by dense, tropical rain forest. To the north and south of the rain forest lie **savannas** and deserts. There are many famous places in Africa. Some are ancient and some are modern. Some are natural wonders and some have been built by humans.

What makes a place famous?

The most common reasons why places become famous are because of their:

- **formation** how they were formed by nature
- **construction** how they were built by humans
- **antiquity** their age, dating back to ancient times
- **size** their height, width, length, volume, or area
- **function** how they work, or what they are used for
- **cultural importance** their value to the customs and society of the country
- **religious importance** their value to the religious beliefs of the country

ZOOM IN
Ancient Egypt, one of the world's first great civilizations, began in Africa more than 5,000 years ago.

Famous places in Africa

Africa has many famous places. Some are built structures and some are features created by nature.

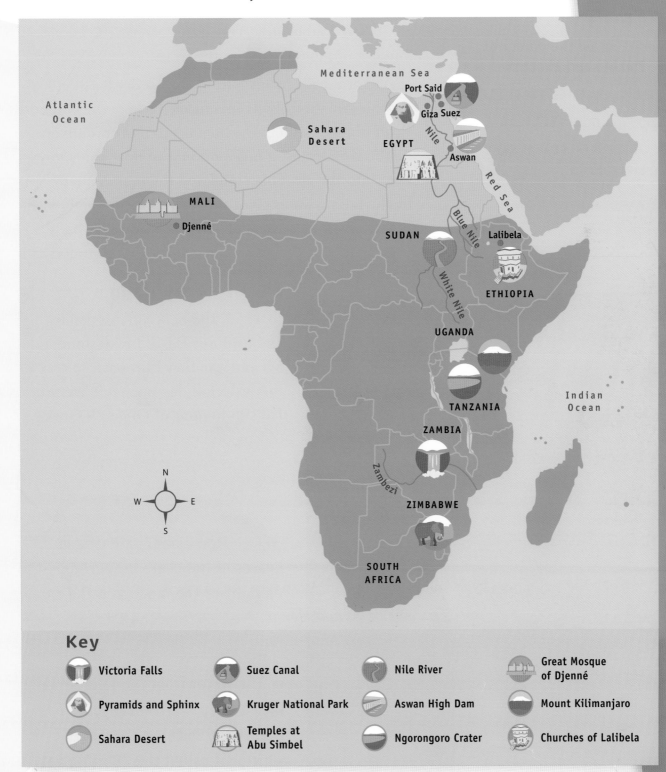

Key

Victoria Falls

Pyramids and Sphinx

Sahara Desert

Suez Canal

Kruger National Park

Temples at Abu Simbel

Nile River

Aswan High Dam

Ngorongoro Crater

Great Mosque of Djenné

Mount Kilimanjaro

Churches of Lalibela

Victoria Falls

ZOOM IN
The spray from the falls can be seen up to 25 miles (40 km) away.

FACT FINDER

Location on the border of Zambia and Zimbabwe

Height up to 420 feet (128 m)

Width 1 mile (1.7 km)

WORLD HERITAGE SITE since 1989

Victoria Falls is a natural feature that is famous for its size and beauty. This waterfall has the largest amount of falling water in the world.

Victoria Falls forms part of the border between Zambia and Zimbabwe. It is formed where the Zambezi River plunges suddenly into a deep, narrow **canyon**. As the river drops, a huge amount of mist and spray rises into the air. This cloud and the roar created by the falling water gives the falls its local name. It is called "Mosi oa tunya," which means "the smoke that thunders."

The first sighting

In 1855, the Scottish missionary and explorer David Livingstone became the first European to reach the waterfall. He named it Victoria Falls in honour of Queen Victoria of England.

ZOOM IN
Moonbows, pale creamy arcs of light, are produced by the light of the moon and the spray from the falls.

◄ The water from the falls flows into a deep, narrow canyon, eventually forming a strong whirlpool called the "Boiling Pot."

6

Road–railway bridge

In 1905 a road–railway bridge was built across the canyon close to the falls. This bridge gives a clear view of the waterfall, which sprays passing trains. The very top of Victoria Falls is made up of three sections, the Eastern Cataract, Rainbow Falls, and the Main Falls.

Victoria Falls is most famous for the great volume of water that occurs in the flood season, from March to May. More than 120 million gallons (550 million l) a minute plunges into the canyon below.

▲ The land near the falls is watered by the spray. The spray creates areas of rain forest that stay bright green all the year round.

Pyramids and Sphinx

FACT FINDER

Location **Giza, Egypt**

Date built **2500 B.C.**

WORLD HERITAGE SITE
since 1979

The pyramids and Sphinx at Giza are built structures that are famous for their size and antiquity. They are the largest stone constructions ever built. The Great Pyramid was the world's tallest building for more than 4000 years.

The pyramids were built as **tombs** for the Egyptian **pharaohs**. The Sphinx was built to guard the pyramids. It has a lion's body to symbolize strength and a human head to symbolize intelligence.

▼ The pyramids were very difficult and dangerous to build. Thousands of laborers died while building them.

ZOOM IN
Each limestone block used in the pyramids weighed about the same as a car.

8

► The Sphinx has several tunnels that go into it as well as under it. No one knows why they are there.

ZOOM IN
The four sides of the Great Pyramid are lined up with the four points of the compass.

The Great Pyramid and Sphinx

The Great Pyramid has several rooms inside to store Pharaoh Khufu's body and possessions. It was built by fitting together more than 2.5 million stone blocks, each weighing about 2 tons (2 tonnes). The Great Pyramid took more than twenty years to build. The Sphinx was carved out of a huge block of solid rock near the pyramids. Its face is thought to be a portrait of Pharaoh Khafre, who was Khufu's son.

Nature and time

The pyramids and the Sphinx have suffered not only from the effects of the sand, wind, and rain over thousands of years, but also from the interference of humans. Today, much more care is taken to help prevent further damage to this famous site.

► In the very middle of the Great Pyramid was the pharaoh's burial chamber, with the queen's below. Other burial chambers and passageways were constructed on the inside, many with false doors to confuse robbers.

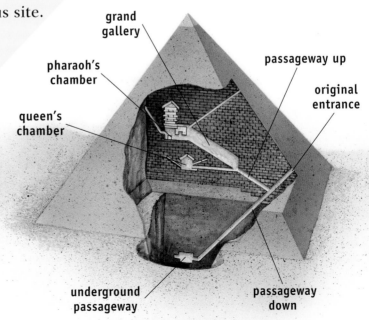

grand gallery

pharaoh's chamber

queen's chamber

passageway up

original entrance

underground passageway

passageway down

Sahara Desert

ZOOM IN
The Sahara is around the same size as the United States of America.

FACT FINDER
Location northern Africa
Size about 3.5 million square miles (9 million sq km)

The Sahara Desert is a natural feature that is famous for its size and climate. It is the largest desert on Earth and is also the hottest. It covers one-third of the African continent. It extends across northern Africa from the Atlantic Ocean to the Red Sea, covering 12 countries.

The Sahara Desert is still growing. It is slowly spreading southwards, as severe droughts and overfarming affect the surrounding area.

▼ The landscape of the Sahara is constantly changing. New sand dunes are created by sandstorms and strong winds.

Shifting sands

Much of the Sahara Desert consists of sand dunes that are moved up to 36 feet (11 m) a year by the wind. Only a few plants and animals are able to live in the hot, dry climate. Some areas have sandstorms for up to 70 days a year. In many parts of the desert, there is less than 10 inches (25 cm) of rainfall a year.

Living in the Sahara

Large areas of the Sahara Desert have no permanent settlements, but there are about 90 large **oases** where people live and grow crops. Most of the Saharan people, such as the Tuareg, are **nomads**. The Tuareg used to cross the desert by camel. These days, many of them use four-wheel-drive vehicles. These cut the journey across this world-famous desert from 15 days or more to just a few days.

▲ Small, fertile areas, called oases, are scattered throughout the Sahara. They offer a resting place for travelers.

ZOOM IN
The highest temperature ever recorded in the world (137.7°F) was in the Sahara in September 1922.

► Camels used to be the only form of transportation across the desert. They used to travel in huge groups known as caravans.

Suez Canal

ZOOM IN
Around 25,000 ships use the Suez Canal each year.

FACT FINDER

Location From Port Said to Suez, Egypt

Length 120 miles (190 km)

Date built 1859–1869

The Suez Canal is a built structure that is famous for its construction and function. This waterway was cut through land so that ships could travel a shorter route from Europe to Asia, without having to sail around Africa. The canal forms a direct link between the Mediterranean Sea and the Red Sea.

A joint project

The Suez Canal was constructed by the Suez Canal Company, which was owned by Egypt and France. The canal took nearly 11 years to build and was opened in 1869. Since then, it has been closed five times for wars and political reasons, but in 1979 the Suez Canal was declared open to every nation.

▼ Over the years the Suez Canal has been made wider and deeper several times to accommodate larger and larger ships.

► The Suez Canal has only one main shipping lane but there is room on either side for other smaller craft to pass.

All one level

The Suez Canal is the longest canal in the world that does not use **locks**, or water lifts, to lift ships from one height or level to another. This means that the canal can be widened and deepened as ships become larger and larger. There are plans to widen it by 2010 so it can be used by supertankers.

The Suez Canal is very important because it is essential for world trade. It is the fastest crossing from the Atlantic Ocean to the Indian Ocean.

ZOOM IN

The Suez Canal shortened the sea route between Britain and India by 6,000 miles (9,700 km), which took weeks off the time of the journey.

INSIDE STORY

In November 1869, the Suez Canal was officially opened with celebrations in Port Said, beginning with fireworks and a ball attended by 6,000 people. Guests included many heads of state, including the French Empress Eugenie, the Emperor of Austria, the Prince of Wales, the Prince of Prussia, and the Prince of the Netherlands. Two convoys of ships entered the canal from its southern and northern points and met at Ismailia, halfway between Port Said and Suez. The parties continued for weeks.

Kruger National Park

Kruger National Park is a natural feature that is famous for its size and function. It is one of the largest national parks in the world and the biggest **game reserve** in South Africa. It was named after Paul Kruger, a president of the South African Republic.

▼ Kruger National Park is home to many animals. Elephants destroy many trees, which affects the other animals and their feeding habits.

ZOOM IN
Park rangers have to undergo special defense training to protect the animals and themselves from heavily armed poachers.

► Although the trade in rhinoceros horn is banned, illegal hunting of rhinoceroses is still a problem in Kruger Park.

Oldest park

Kruger National Park is the oldest national park in South Africa. It is a **biosphere reserve**, however, the **poaching** of animals in the park for their skins, horns, and ivory is still a serious problem. South African **conservationists** now **de-horn** rhinoceroses in the hope that it will stop illegal hunting.

Animals galore

The park has one of the largest varieties of mammals in any African park or reserve. As well as lions, buffaloes, rhinoceroses, leopards, and elephants, the park supports more than 3,000 different **species** of **fauna** and **flora**.

To conserve the park, rangers have had to limit the numbers of animals, particularly elephants. They do this by either moving the young and healthy ones to other reserves, or by **culling**, or putting down, the sick and elderly ones. Kruger National Park is one of the world's leading centers of wildlife research.

ZOOM IN
Tourists have to stay in fenced camps and are only allowed to travel between sunrise and sunset. They must stay on the sealed roads and not get out of their vehicles.

Temples at Abu Simbel

ZOOM IN
Ramses II had five wives and 100 children.

FACT FINDER

Location southeast Egypt

Date built 1200 B.C. (around 3,200 years ago)

WORLD HERITAGE SITE since 1979

The temples at Abu Simbel are built structures that are famous for their construction, cultural importance and antiquity. These magnificent temples were built by Pharaoh Ramses II as monuments to himself and to his family.

Building the temples

The Great Temple and the Small Temple were made by cutting directly into the solid rock of the cliff face and then hollowing out a huge space behind the face for the inside rooms. They took more than 20 years to complete.

In the 1960s, the temples were cut into more than 1,000 blocks and transported 200 feet (60 m) up the cliff face. They were reassembled there so they would not be covered by the waters of the new Aswan High Dam.

▼ Four statues of Ramses II and two of his wife, Nefertari, guard the entrance to the Small Temple.

► The Great Temple is thought to be the most beautiful of all Ramses II's temples. At the entrance, each statue of the pharaoh is 65 feet (20 m) high.

◄ Inside the Great Temple is the Great Hall of Pillars. The walls and ceilings are brightly painted.

The two temples

At the entrance of the Great Temple are four huge statues of the pharaoh, sitting. At his feet are statues of his family. Inside is the Great Hall of Pillars. A series of passageways and chambers extends 180 feet (55 m) inside the cliff. The Small Temple is dedicated both to Ramses' first queen, Nefertari, and to Hathor, the goddess of love.

The temples at Abu Simbel are lasting monuments to the great power and far-reaching influence of Ramses II.

INSIDE STORY

The Greater Abu Simbel Temple (or Sun Temple) was built so precisely that only twice a year, the rays from the morning sun reach through the entrance and down the Great Hall of Statues, lighting up the four statues at the back wall. These two days coincide with the pharaoh's birthday on February 21 and his coronation on October 22.

Nile River

FACT FINDER

Location northeast Africa from Uganda to the Mediterranean Sea

Length 4,160 miles (6,695 km)

▼ The Nile River flows northwards from its source in Uganda, then through Sudan into Egypt.

The Nile River is a natural feature that is famous for its size and function. It is the longest river in the world. It begins as the White Nile in Uganda and is joined in Sudan by the Blue Nile. The two rivers form one large river called the Nile River.

Mud and silt

For hundreds of years, the farmers planted their crops in the mud and **silt** on the banks of the Nile River and its valley. This mud and silt were left behind by the **annual** flooding of the Nile River.

The valley and the **Nile Delta**, which is where the river meets the sea, are among the most fertile farming areas in the world.

◄ The upper Nile River is home to hippopotomuses, crocodiles and many types of fish.

Farming and transportation

Many cities and towns grew up along the Nile River because it was so important to farming and transportation. The early Egyptians depended on it as their chief transportation route, especially during the flood season when the roads were under water.

These days, with air and rail transportation and the construction of highways, the Nile River is no longer vital as a means of transportation. However, it is still important in parts of Sudan during the flood season when steam boats on the Nile are the only reliable transport. This famous river is still essential to the livelihood of the people of Africa.

► Many thousands of people travel up and down the Nile River every day, including villagers, fishermen, and farmers.

Aswan High Dam

The Aswan High Dam is a built structure that is famous for its size and function. It is built across the Nile River and is one of the largest dams ever built. The Aswan High Dam provides electricity for Egyptian homes and industries, as well as water for **irrigation** of their farms. It also protects the crops and the people from floods.

▼ The Aswan High Dam was built using layers of packed sand, gravel, dirt, and rocks.

▼ The Aswan High Dam replaced the first, smaller Aswan Dam, which stands nearby and is used chiefly to generate electricity.

ZOOM IN
Enough rock was used in construction of the dam to build 18 of the pyramids at Giza.

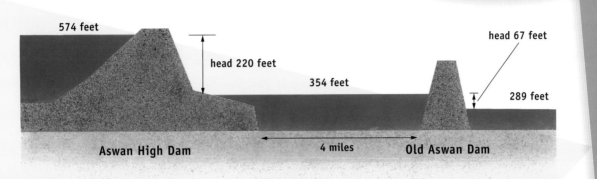

574 feet

head 220 feet

354 feet

head 67 feet

289 feet

Aswan High Dam

4 miles

Old Aswan Dam

Using the floods

Before the Aswan High Dam was built, the Nile River flooded every year, leaving behind rich mud that the farmers used to plant their crops. These days, the dam holds some of the water back in Lake Nasser so there are no floods. The dam then releases it in the dry season when it is needed. Before, the floods allowed only one crop a year. Now, up to three crops a year can be harvested in some areas.

Environmental problems

The Aswan High Dam has led to some serious environmental problems. Now that the land is not fertilized by the silt left behind by the floodwaters of the Nile River, farmers have to use chemical fertilizers. However, the dam is world famous for the improvements it made to the everyday life of the Egyptian people.

▲ The building of the Aswan High Dam has evened out the flow of the Nile River all year round.

ZOOM IN
In order to build the dam, many towns, villages, ancient temples, tombs, and archeological sites had to be moved. Others were left to be covered by the rising waters.

Ngorongoro Crater

▼ In the center of Ngorongoro crater is Lake Magadi.

Ngorongoro Crater is a natural landform that is famous for its size and formation. It is the world's sixth largest **caldera**, or volcanic crater. It is the largest caldera in the world with an unbroken rim. It was once an **active volcano**. But after it erupted more than 2 million years ago, it collapsed back into itself, leaving a huge crater.

Protected land

Ngorongoro Crater is an area where animal and plant life are protected. It is made up of many different types of **habitat**. They are open grasslands and savannas, woodlands, swamps, lakes, and rivers. These support about 30,000 animals, which is one of the largest collections of wildlife in the world.

Animals all year

Most of the Ngorongoro animals stay in the crater all year round because there is always water available, even in the dry season. Unfortunately, poaching has affected the animal population, particularly the rhinoceroses.

Ngorongoro Crater has a number of **soda lakes**, which are formed by underground spring water bubbling up through the soda layers in the earth. Although this makes the water very salty, these lakes are home to millions of flamingos and other water birds.

▶ The Ngorongoro Crater is a haven for many types of animals, including zebras and flamingos.

ZOOM IN
Even in the dry season, there is enough food in the crater to feed 2 million animals.

ZOOM IN
You can fly by small plane onto an airstrip that is right on the crater's rim.

◀ To conserve the crater and its wildlife, the Masai people of the area are allowed to use it for grazing only a limited number of cattle.

Great Mosque of Djenné

The Great Mosque of Djenné is a built structure that is famous for its size and construction. It is the world's largest mud-brick building. It was built on top of the ruins of the first Great Mosque, which was built around 1240. The only part still remaining from the first mosque is a small, walled section containing a grave site that was used for the burial of important leaders of the city.

Mud bricks

The Great Mosque is built from sun-dried bricks held together by mud **mortar** and then plastered over with mud. The walls are massive. Some are up to 2 feet (60 cm) thick. This thickness is needed to hold up the weight of the building and to help keep out the sun's heat.

ZOOM IN

Loudspeakers have been installed in the mosque, but the people have resisted modern improvements, such as tiled floors, plumbing, and electricity.

◄ The area in front of the Great Mosque is a huge market place, the social center of the town.

minarets

▲ The Great Mosque is built on a raised, walled, mud platform to protect it from the floodwaters of the nearby river.

Tall and impressive

The Great Mosque stands five stories high. Half of it is covered by a roof with pillars and shrines on top, and the other half is an open prayer hall. The front of the Great Mosque has three **minarets**, or prayer towers, which overlook the busy market that is held every week.

Because the Great Mosque is built from mud, it is damaged by the sun and rain. Every year, the local people replaster the walls with mud from the nearby river to protect this world-famous building.

ZOOM IN
Non-Muslims have been banned from entering the mosque since 1996 when the behavior of a fashion magazine photographer offended local religious leaders.

Mount Kilimanjaro

Mount Kilimanjaro is a natural landform that is famous for its size. It is the highest mountain in Africa. Mount Kilimanjaro is made up of three separate volcanoes, Shira, Kibo, and Mawenzi. None of these is still active. Mount Kilimanjaro's **summit** is capped by snow and ice all year.

▼ The shiny ice caps of Mount Kilimanjaro can be seen for many miles across the hot African savannas.

► The slopes of Mount Kilimanjaro have dense forests.

The three volcanoes

The oldest volcano, Shira, stopped erupting and collapsed into itself about 500,000 years ago. Kibo, the highest and youngest volcano, and Mawenzi continued to erupt. The lava from them joined to form a ridge that connected their two peaks. Mawenzi died out about 200,000 years ago, but Kibo is lying **dormant**. It is not **extinct**. Recent research has shown that there is volcanic activity within Kibo, and that molten lava is just 1,300 feet (400 m) below the summit crater.

Problems ahead

Some scientists believe that Kibo is warming up again, while others believe that **global warming** is responsible for the ice cap melting in recent years. It has been predicted that Mount Kilimanjaro's ice cap may disappear completely by about 2014.

Churches of Lalibela

FACT FINDER

Location **Lalibela, Ethiopia**

Date built **1200s**

WORLD HERITAGE SITE
since 1978

The churces of Lalibela are built structures that are famous for their construction and religious importance. The 11 churches were cut out of solid rock. Their fame brought many people to Lalibela and made it the religious centre of Ethiopia in the 1200s.

The churches took 24 years to build. The local people believed that angels must have built the churches at night, because they were built so quickly.

ZOOM IN
The rock churches are connected underground by tunnels that even go underneath a river.

▼ People use walkways to get across the deep trench that surrounds the base of some of the churches.

walkway

► The Bieta Giorgis church is set in a deep pit, and if viewed from above, is shaped like a cross.

trench

Carved in stone

The churches were built in three different ways. Some churches were built inside a natural cave. Others were cut into a cliff face, sometimes widening an existing cave. The most famous churches were cut from the rock in one piece and separated all around by a trench. They are attached to the surrounding rock only by their bases.

Guardians of the churches

The churches are cared for by priests who guard the precious artistic and religious treasures. The most famous church, Bieta Giorgis, is set apart from the others. The priests make sure these churches are preserved for the future.

Famous places of Africa

Our world has a rich collection of famous places. Some are spectacular natural wonders and some are engineering or architectural masterpieces. These famous places in Africa are outstanding in many different ways.

Wonders formed by nature

PLACE	FAMOUS FOR
Victoria Falls	The largest body of falling water in the world
Sahara Desert	The largest desert in the world The hottest desert in the world
Kruger National Park	One of the oldest game reserves in the world One of the largest game reserves in the world
Nile River	The longest river in the world
Ngorongoro Crater	One of the largest calderas in the world The largest caldera in the world with an unbroken rim
Mount Kilimanjaro	The highest mountain in Africa One of the largest volcanos in the world

Masterpieces built by humans

PLACE	FAMOUS FOR
Pyramids and Sphinx at Giza	Great Pyramid is largest stone building in the world Sphinx is carved from a single ridge of solid rock
Suez Canal	The first link between the Mediterranean Sea and the Red Sea
Temples at Abu Simbel	Ancient monuments to Pharaoh Ramses II and his family carved into a rock cliff
Aswan High Dam	One of the largest structures ever built
Great Mosque of Djenné	The largest mud-brick building in the world
Churches of Lalibela	Churches carved out of solid rock, all completely below the level of the ground

Glossary

active volcano a volcano that is able to erupt at any time

annual happening once a year

biosphere reserve an area where animal and plant life are protected

caldera a large crater formed by a volcanic eruption

canyon a deep valley with steep sides

conservationists people who work to make sure that animal and plant life are not destroyed

continent one of the main land masses of the world

culling removing or killing animals in order to control their numbers so as not to harm the environment

de-horn to remove the horn from an animal

dormant not active, resting

extinct no longer existing

fauna the animals that live in a particular area

flora the plants of a particular area

game reserve an area set aside for the preservation of wild animals

global warming the rise in temperature of the whole of the Earth's atmosphere or air

habitat an animal's natural living place

irrigation the supply of water to an area, usually by a system of canals

locks parts of a canal with gates at each end allowing ships to be raised or lowered from one level to another

minarets tall towers built on a Muslim mosque, from which an official calls the people to prayer

mortar a mixture used for joining bricks together

Nile Delta flat, very fertile land near the mouth of the Nile River

nomads people who wander from place to place hunting, gathering food, and grazing their animals

oases places in a desert where there is water and plants can grow

pharaohs ancient Egyptian kings

poaching hunting animals illegally from someone else's land

savannas grassland regions scattered with trees

silt earth-like material, like mud, which is first carried and then left behind by running water

soda lakes lakes formed by hot underground springs that bubble up to Earth's surface

species a group of animals or plants that can reproduce their own kind

summit the top, or highest point

tombs graves, especially for important people

Index